BARNARD CASTLE

County Durham

❖

EGGLESTONE ABBEY

North Yorkshire

❖

BOWES CASTLE

North Yorkshire

❖

Katy Kenyon

❖ CONTENTS ❖

BARNARD CASTLE
INTRODUCTION
TOUR AND DESCRIPTION
4 Town Ward
7 Middle Ward
8 Outer Ward
9 Inner Ward
HISTORY
14 The Baliol family
17 The Beauchamps
18 The Nevills
18 Sieges
20 Later history

EGGLESTONE ABBEY
INTRODUCTION
TOUR AND DESCRIPTION
22 The church
25 The cloister
26 East range
28 North range
28 West range
HISTORY
30 Poverty
31 Life in the abbey
32 The suppression of the monastery
32 Later history

BOWES CASTLE
TOUR AND DESCRIPTION
HISTORY

Published by English Heritage
23 Savile Row, London W1X 1AB
© English Heritage 1999
First published by English Heritage 1999
Photographs, unless otherwise specified, were taken by English Heritage
Photographic Unit, and remain the copyright of English Heritage

Edited by Lorimer Poultney
Designed by Pauline Hull
Printed in England by Sterling
LP C50 FA6965 ISBN 1 85074 720 2

BARNARD CASTLE
INTRODUCTION

❖

ARNARD CASTLE commands a strategic site overlooking the River Tees. For over two centuries it was the principal stronghold of the Baliol family, who founded the town at its gates and turned the castle into one of the largest fortresses in northern England. By the thirteenth century, however, the family had lost the estate and it had passed into the hands of the Beauchamp family, Earls of Warwick, and later to the Crown. It never again regained the importance it had held for the Baliols and suffered years of neglect. It played a major role in national events during the sixteenth century, holding out for eleven days during a siege in 1569, but by this time it was practically ruinous.

Barnard Castle, watercolour by Thomas Hearne, 1788

TOUR AND DESCRIPTION

❖

The foundation of Barnard Castle dates from the twelfth century, when Guy de Baliol built a timber castle here. He chose this particular site for a number of

The castle's strong defensive position on the river cliff above the River Tees

reasons. It was naturally defended on two sides by steep cliffs and the River Tees, while to the north of the site there was a road, and a ford over the river, both laid out by the Romans. Finally, positioned between upland and lowland areas, it was close to good farming land, forests and the river, which could supply the castle with most of its provisions. Guy established the castle, but it was his nephew Bernard and his son, another Bernard, who turned the castle into the major fortress you can see today: 'Bernard's Castle'. They rebuilt the castle in stone and enlarged the site, enclosing it with a curtain wall. They also divided the area into four enclosures, known as wards.

TOWN WARD

The name of this area probably comes from the use of the ward by the townspeople and their livestock for protection during times of trouble.

The ward would have housed a wide range of activities associated with the day-to-day running of the castle and

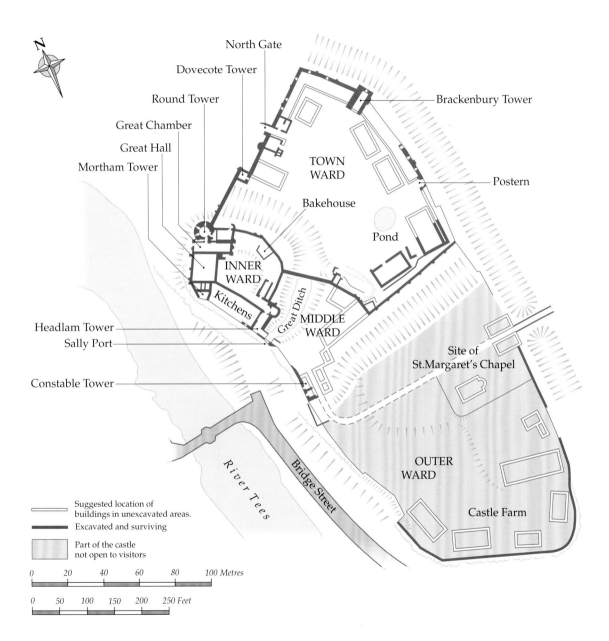

North Gate

Dovecote Tower

Round Tower

Great Chamber

Great Hall

Mortham Tower

Brackenbury Tower

TOWN WARD

Postern

Bakehouse

Pond

INNER WARD

Kitchens

Great Ditch

MIDDLE WARD

Headlam Tower

Sally Port

Site of
St. Margaret's Chapel

Constable Tower

River Tees

Bridge Street

OUTER WARD

Castle Farm

Suggested location of
buildings in unexcavated areas.

Excavated and surviving

Part of the castle
not open to visitors

0   20   40   60   80   100 Metres

0   50   100   150   200   250 Feet

estate, with stores and accommodation for men, animals and supplies. Originally there were buildings ranged around the walls, with one or more central courtyards. At the southern end of the ward, archaeological work has revealed the remains of two of these buildings. A cobbled passage between them led to a pond, once stocked with fish for the lord's table.

In the north-west corner of the ward is the **Dovecot Tower** with the remains of nesting boxes inside. Pigeons were used as a source of fresh meat. The young pigeons, or 'squabs', and eggs were collected using either a 'potence', a central revolving pole with ladders fixed to it, or a scaffold of beams fixed to the walls. There were some more nesting

❖ DOVECOTES ❖

Having a dovecote was a privilege, available only to the lord of the manor. There was not enough grain to keep many animals over the winter so fresh meat was in short supply. Pigeons, and other wild animals and birds, were a welcome source of fresh meat. Oliver de Serres wrote in 1600 that 'no man need ever have an ill-provisioned house if there be but attached to it a dovecot, a warren and a fishpond wherein meat may be found as readily at hand as if it were stored in a larder'.

The pigeons were not just kept for meat. The dung was potent and was recommended for growing hops and barley, and was used in tanning to soften leather hides. It was also used in various remedies, for example bird's dung and watercress was used as a cure for baldness and gout. Feathers and down were used to fill pillows and beds; it was a common superstition that those who slept on pigeon feathers would live to a good age. The birds could also be used as message carriers in times of war and peace, and as prey for the lord's falcons.

Homing pigeons were used to carry messages

boxes in the curtain wall to the left of the tower.

To the north of the tower is the **North Gatehouse,** originally a two-storey building, with a central gate passage. The room to the right was probably the porter's lodge. In the room to the left are sewer pits for two 'garderobes', or toilets. Garderobes were not flushed by water; instead, a stone or wooden seat with a hole was set over a chute which emptied into a pit outside.

At the east side of the ward is the **Brackenbury Tower**. The lower storey was used as a store room and living quarters. Inside is a garderobe at the end of a short passage. To the right of the building are the original stairs to the first floor. The upper room was more comfortable and may have provided accommodation for a more senior member of the household. The window seat, which originally looked out onto the market place, was added at a later date.

MIDDLE WARD

The Middle Ward was also known as 'Many Gates' for the simple reason that there are three gates to it. It would have contained accommodation for some of the castle's higher-ranking officers, and probably the stables.

The entrance from the Town Ward was guarded by a gatehouse, a simple rectangular building, and a drawbridge, which passed over a

Print from 1829 showing the Inner Ward seen from a causeway that had filled up the great ditch

short, water-filled moat. Beneath the modern bridge are two large buttresses, which supported the pivot of the bridge, and a hole which received the counterweight as it closed. To the right of the bridge is a small dam, built to stop the moat draining into the dry ditch around the Inner Ward. To the left are the remains of a square angle tower. All of these defensive measures were added in the fourteenth century. Two garderobe chutes, which emptied into the moat through arched sewers, are visible at the base of the wall.

At the other side of the ward is the **Constable Tower**, which guarded the original main route into the castle. The tower was three storeys high. On the ground floor were two rooms on either side of a central gate passage. The rooms of the upper floors provided accommodation for the constable. Castles were 'empty' much of the time as the lord and his household were often away on business, at other estates or at the royal court. The constable, usually a great man himself, was the person appointed by the lord to administer the castle in the lord's absence.

Underneath the tower are two deep, rock-cut pits used to drain the ditch at the front of the ward.

OUTER WARD

(not open to the public – private land)
The gatehouse in the Outer Ward was originally the main route into the castle. Beside the gate was St Margaret's Chapel. Castles usually had a communal chapel or church,

Reconstruction by Terry Ball of how the castle may have appeared in the fifteenth century

as well as smaller chapels for private worship. Placing the chapel by the main entrance enabled travellers to pray for a good journey or give thanks for their safe return.

The Outer Ward was also the site of the 'demesne' farm. It was usual for a lord to keep some of his land to be worked for profit and to supply the castle with provisions; this land was known as the demesne land. In 1327, Edward III, who held the castle at that time, was still farming the demesne lands. Records show that he employed a number of people on the farm. They were all paid in kind, receiving an allowance of corn. The townspeople were obliged to help with ploughing and harvesting for several days each year.

INNER WARD

The Inner Ward was the main residential area for the lord. It was heavily defended by a wide rock-cut ditch, high curtain wall and a formidable **Gatehouse**. There have been series of gatehouses on the site, each of greater military strength than the one before. By the fourteenth century, a three-storey tower with a 'demi-bastion' (a semi-circular tower projecting into the ditch) guarded the entrance.

To the left of the gate passage is the **Headlam Tower**. This is the site of the original gatehouse built in the early twelfth century, later converted into the three-storey tower, with

residential chambers on its upper floors. To the right of the passage was a narrow rectangular building, added in the fourteenth century when the defences were updated. It is believed to have been a porter's lodge or guardhouse.

Nothing remains of the **kitchens,** but fifteenth- and sixteenth-century documents describe a three-storey block containing apartments and the main kitchens. Kitchens were the centre of a complex of sculleries, slaughterhouses, larders and other rooms. Food was originally cooked on open, central hearths, but these were generally replaced by huge wall fireplaces, big enough to roast a whole ox. Kitchens were hot and dirty places, and usually had high ceilings to let the smoke escape through the roof.

At the end of the kitchen block is the **Mortham Tower**, built mainly in the fourteenth century to provide more residential space. In the fifteenth century a garderobe turret was built on to the upper three storeys. At the base of the tower are two rooms known as the 'buttery' and 'pantry', where bread, beer and candles were stored. The word pantry comes from the French word '*pain*' meaning bread, while buttery comes from '*bouteille*' meaning bottle. Between these two rooms was a short passage to the kitchen, where food would have been collected from a serving hatch and carried into the Great Hall.

Great Hall

The hall was the central point of the estate and was often a very grand building, displaying the wealth and power of the lord. It was used for meals and feasts, entertaining guests and conducting estate business. The room would have been open to the high beamed roof. In the centre, an open hearth heated the room, although this was probably replaced at a later date by a wall fireplace. The windows, dating from the fourteenth century, would have been glazed by this period, and have wooden shutters. Across the upper end of the hall, on a raised platform or 'dais' was the lord's table. The lord sat here is great state, surrounded by rich decoration and displays of gold and silver plate. Three joist holes in the wall above the dais show the position of a gallery. The household sat in the main body of the hall on benches or stools, at simple tables made out of boards and trestles.

Great Chamber

Off the upper end of the hall was the Great Chamber. The ground floor room was used for storage but had a domestic use as well. Every household was practically self-sufficient, but what could not be produced from the manor lands was bought at annual fairs and stored until needed. Items of special value could be kept under the Great Chamber, close to the lord.

The upper room was reached by an external stone staircase. This room, and the Round Tower, were the private quarters of the lord. Great chambers were used as bed-sitting rooms for sleeping, playing games, receiving visitors and occasional meals. There was little furniture, the main item being a large bed hung with curtains, which could be drawn at night to give some privacy, as lesser servants often slept in their master's room. Otherwise there were chests for the lord's valuables and clothes, a few 'perches', or wooden pegs for clothes, and stools. The oriel window overlooking the river was added in the fifteenth

A copy of a fifteenth-century illustration of a wedding feast in a great hall. Excavations at Barnard Castle revealed the debris of one such feast that had blocked the kitchen drains

AKG, LONDON

❖ DECORATION ❖

Castles were originally highly decorated, and not the grim forbidding stone walls we usually see today. Outside walls were often white-washed and roofs were sometimes covered with lead cresting and ornamental figures of knights.

Internal walls were brightly painted or covered with tapestries or wooden panelling.

Decoration was normally painted onto a white or colour-washed background. A common motif was the use of red lines to represent stonework;

BRITISH LIBRARY

within each 'block' ornaments such as flowers were then painted. Religious, historical and allegorical subjects were popular, painted in circles. By the late thirteenth century the hanging of painted shields was customary.

Alternatively, tapestries, embroidered or painted wall-cloths, lined the walls, hung from hooks. Heraldic tapestries were particularly popular and were often placed behind the lord's table. Curtains and hangings were also used to divide rooms and to keep

How hangings were used to line walls and subdivide rooms. Notice the glazed windows and wooden shutters

out draughts. Bare boards and trestles would have been covered with carpets and cushions.

century, possibly by Richard, Duke of Gloucester (later Richard III), as above the window is a carving of a boar, which was his emblem.

Round Tower

From the fourteenth century onwards, great chambers were used as private dining rooms and the bed was moved to separate sleeping quarters. The Round Tower held the principal bed chamber for the lord, with direct access from the Great Chamber. The second floor may have been for the lady of the castle, as a sixteenth-century document refers to this room as 'My Lady's Chamber'. The large square windows, which replaced three arrow loops, were added in the fifteenth or sixteenth centuries. The third, rather spartan, floor probably had a military use and had direct access to the battlements. In the event of an attack, the floors below could be closed off by a door at the head of the stairs and locked and bolted from inside. All the floors and the roof of the tower were removed in the eighteenth century when the owner converted it into a shot tower.

The basement was used as a storeroom and had a domestic use, as there is a well. The three arrow slits have 'fish-tail' bases which allowed the archers to direct their fire at the base of the tower outside. There is an unusual spiral pattern on the ceiling.

The Great Hall, Great Chamber and Round Tower, with the Mortham Tower on the left

Other buildings

The name of the **Prison Tower** comes from sixteenth-century documents and it is not certain if it were ever used for this purpose. Prisoners in castles included local offenders and common criminals awaiting trial; imprisonment itself was not used as a legal punishment. Castles could also hold high-ranking political prisoners, but they would not be held in a prison, but in rooms within the castle suited to their status.

To the right of the tower are traces of the original battlements and steps to the wall walk.

In front of the Prison Tower is the **Bakehouse** with the remains of ovens. The stone-lined hole was either a cistern or a cold store for food. Baking was often done in a separate building, usually about once a week. Many people were too poor to have their own oven and could take their dough to the lord's bakehouse for a small fee.

The **Postern Tower** provides access to the 'berm', the area directly beneath the curtain wall, above the great ditch. At the end of the ditch, beneath the bridge to the Inner Ward, is an arch with a portcullis. This is known as a 'sally-port'. A counter-attack, or 'sally' was a useful method of defence and gates like this one were used to spring surprise attacks on the enemy. This particular gate would also have allowed a party of mounted knights to make a rapid defence of the bridge below.

❖ DEFENDING THE CASTLE ❖

❖ For those inside the castle, war did not come without warning. At the first sign of trouble, the castle would be put on a war footing. Supplies were gathered and a garrison assembled.

❖ Any force attacking a castle had a number of weapons and tactics it could use. Large catapults and cross-bows, known as siege engines, would batter the walls with missiles. Moveable towers, or 'belfries', allowed attackers to fire over the walls while ladders were used to scale them. Protected by screens, men could lever out stones in the walls, or even undermine them to make them collapse.

❖ Defending archers would harass the enemy and make it as difficult as possible for them to reach the walls. Projecting wall towers allowed the outer face and the base of the wall to be defended without the defenders exposing themselves to attack.

❖ The broad ditches were intended to stop belfies being pushed up to the walls. In order to cross them, the ditches could be filled with brushwood, logs and stones. Defenders would bombard the attackers and if a belfry reached the walls they would try to push it over or set it alight.

But no castle could defend itself against attack without supplies. If food and water were cut off, the castle, no matter how strong its defences, would eventually surrender.

Attacking a castle: a detail from a fourteenth-century manuscript. Note the catapult and the archer on the tower

BRIDGEMAN ART LIBRARY, LONDON

HISTORY

❖

Seals of the Baliol family.
From the top: Bernard de
Baliol I, Hugh de Baliol,
and John de Baliol II

THE HISTORY OF BARNARD CASTLE is set against a background of troubles. Throughout the medieval period, the North was a remote outpost, dogged by rebellion and frequent raids by the Scots. There was also a simmering dispute between the powerful Bishops of Durham and the Crown over ownership of the castle. The land on which Barnard Castle was built had been given to the Church in the ninth century, but by the eleventh century had been forcibly taken by the Earls of Northumberland. The land reverted back to the Crown at the end of the eleventh century after William II crushed a rebellion by the Earl, and in 1095 the king granted the land to Guy de Baliol, a loyal supporter from Picardy in north-eastern France. The Church believed that the king had no right to do this as the land rightfully belonged to it.

THE BALIOL FAMILY

Although Guy held the lands around Barnard Castle for thirty years, little is known about him, probably because his achievements were overshadowed by those of his nephew, Bernard de Baliol. Bernard succeeded in 1125 and, together with his younger son, Bernard de Baliol II, rebuilt and expanded the original earthwork castle. He also founded the town outside the castle walls that now bears his name, and gave it its first charter. The charters made by Bernard and successive members of the family granted a market and set out a system of town fields, pastures and moorlands, and set aside demesne lands and a hunting park for their own use.

Trouble on the Scottish border was never far away, and Bernard fought against King David I of Scotland at the Battle of the Standard at Cowton Moor in 1138. Bernard died in 1155 and was succeeded by his eldest son Guy, who died in 1162. Guy's brother Bernard de Baliol II inherited the estates and held them until 1199. He left no male heir and was somehow succeeded by Eustace de Helicourt, a member of a local tenant family, who changed his name to Baliol on his succession.

By the early thirteenth century the family seems to have fallen into financial difficulties, perhaps because of all the money spent on building the castle. In about 1190 Bishop Pudsey of Durham held the castle in security for a loan made to Eustace. The castle may not have been returned to the family until as late as 1212 when King John ordered the castle to be returned to Eustace's son Hugh.

Hugh de Baliol had succeeded in 1205. As a close ally of King John, Hugh defended the North in 1216 against the Northumbrian barons, who were in open revolt supported by Alexander I of Scotland. King John came north to restore order, but after he left Alexander advanced, and

The castle from across the River Tees. You can see how the castle dominated the strategic river crossing. The ford was replaced by the bridge probably in the fourteenth century

in July Barnard was besieged. While riding around the castle, Eustace de Vesci, Alexander's brother-in-law, was killed by a crossbow bolt. A sixteenth-century account says that 'one within discharged a cross bowe, and strake Eustace Vesey... on the forehead with such might, that he fell dead to the ground.' The siege is not well documented, but seems to have been unsuccessful. It also delayed the barons long enough to allow John to return to the offensive.

Hugh died in 1228, and was succeeded by his son, John de Baliol, possibly the most successful member of the family. Through his marriage to Devorguilla of Galloway, he gained land and titles, becoming one of the wealthiest men in Britain. He ruthlessly imprisoned Devorguilla's illegitimate brother Thomas in the castle from 1235 to 1296 to ensure his hold on his Scottish lands. John was a loyal supporter of Henry III and fought for him at the Battle of Lewes in 1264 against the rebellious barons. He was captured and the castle was briefly held by the barons to ensure that John kept the peace.

Engraving by le-Kaux, published in 1845, of the north side of the Inner Ward. The 'monk' was an eccentric recluse who lived in the Round Tower and acted as self-appointed guide.

John died in 1269. His widow, Devorguilla, was devoted to his memory, for which she founded Sweetheart Abbey, near Dumfries, in 1273. She kept John's embalmed heart, in a casket, with her throughout her widowhood. At mealtimes, food would be served as if John still sat at high table, and distributed to the poor afterwards. She died in 1290 and was buried at Sweetheart Abbey together with John's heart.

John left three sons. In 1278, the youngest son, John de Baliol II, succeeded. In 1290, because of the titles inherited from his father, he became a contender for the vacant throne of Scotland. A council of Scottish and English lords, convened by Edward I, chose John as the new king. He swore loyalty to Edward, but once he was on the throne he rejected the authority of the English king. In 1296 war broke out and Edward marched to Scotland. John, fearing for his life, surrendered his right to the throne and was imprisoned in the Tower of London. All of his English estates were confiscated. On his release he retired to his Picardy estates, all that remained to the Baliol family.

During these upheavals Bishop Anthony Bek took possession of the castle and lordship, claiming the Church's right to the castle. The king tolerated this for a while, but claimed the castle back in 1306.

THE BEAUCHAMPS

In 1307, on his deathbed, the king granted the lordship to Guy de Beauchamp, Earl of Warwick, one of his most outstanding war captains. The Beauchamps were rarely in residence, their main interests being in the Midlands, and they used the castle mostly as a source of revenue. The outer wards were largely abandoned, making the castle smaller and cheaper to run. Contemporary accounts and surveys reveal the slow deterioration of the buildings. On the other hand, the defences and buildings of the Inner and Middle Wards were modernised and improved. At this time the North was under even greater threat from the Scots, after their success at the battle of Bannockburn in 1314. Barnard was kept on a war footing until events calmed down after 1322.

Guy died in 1315 and was succeeded by his son Thomas, who was only two years old. During his minority the castle and estates were held by the Crown. The bishops petitioned in Parliament for the return of Barnard Castle, but Edward III made it clear that the earls would not be removed. Thomas de Beauchamp came of age in 1330, and held the estate until his death in 1369. Thomas was succeeded by his son Thomas de Beauchamp II, but during his lifetime Thomas obtained permission from Henry IV to transfer the ownership of the estate to his son Richard.

Stone effigy of Devorguilla (now sadly headless) from Sweetheart Abbey showing her holding John Baliol's heart

HISTORIC SCOTLAND

Badge with Richard III's emblem, the boar, found at Middleham Castle in North Yorkshire

Richard held the estate until his death in 1439, but spent little money on the castle. In 1440, Bishop Nevill, 'with a great multitude and in a manner of riot and war', seized the castle, but the king intervened and the castle was returned. Richard was succeeded by his son Henry, who was a minor, so the estate was once more in the hands of the Crown. Henry came of age in 1445, but died a year later, leaving an infant daughter Anne, who herself died at the age of five in 1449.

THE NEVILLS

The castle now passed to Henry's sister Anne, who was married to Richard Nevill, a member of that powerful northern family. Nevill gained the title of Earl of Warwick, and is better known to history as the 'Kingmaker' for his role in the Wars of the Roses. After Richard Nevill's death at the battle of Barnet in 1471 the bishops once again tried to recover possession of the castle. Instead, completely disregarding the just claims of Anne, the lordship passed to Richard, Duke of Gloucester, her son-in-law.

In 1483 Richard became king. He was popular in the North, and showed great interest in the castle, making alterations and plans, although most were never realised because of his early death at Bosworth Field in 1485. Anne Nevill was restored to her estates, but she granted them to Henry VII for his lifetime, on the condition that they were ultimately returned to her successors. This agreement was never respected and the castle stayed in royal hands until 1603. During this time the castle's general decline continued, and surveys comment on its dilapidation and make constant requests for money to pay for repairs.

SIEGES

Despite the decline in its fortunes, the castle made its most notable contribution to national events during the sixteenth century. Many people, particularly in the North, were unhappy with the new Protestant religion and openly rebelled against it.

Richard III

SOCIETY OF ANTIQUARIES OF LONDON

In 1536, Robert Bowes, the constable of Barnard, was forced to surrender the castle to rebels from Richmond, mainly because he was unable to trust his own men who sympathised with the rebels. But the rebel success was short-lived. The uprising was crushed and the leader hanged at Richmond in 1537.

In 1569, the 'Rising of the North', a plan to depose Elizabeth I and replace her with Mary, Queen of Scots and restore the Catholic faith, once again threatened the castle. The Rising centred around the earls of Westmorland and Northumberland, both powerful figures in the North. Sir George Bowes, a trusted servant of the Crown and a Protestant, hearing of the rebellion, went to Barnard and stocked it with provisions and men. On 2 December 1569, 5,000 rebels appeared outside the castle. The nearest assistance was

The deep rock-cut ditch surrounding the Inner Ward

still being assembled at York by the Earl of Sussex, Lord President of the Council of the North. On 8 December, the walls of the Outer Ward were breached in two places and the Town Ward taken soon after. The defenders retreated into the Inner Ward, but their water supply was cut off.

Many of the soldiers were unreliable. By 12 December men were leaping over the walls in great numbers. Sir George later wrote that: 'I fownde the people in the castle in continuall mutenyes... in one daye and nyght, two hundred and twenty six men laepyd over the walles, and opened the gaytes, and went to the enemy; off which nomber, thirty fyve broke their necks, legges or arms in the leaping.' This forced a surrender and Sir George was allowed to march out of the castle with four hundred of his loyal men. The castle was lost, but thanks to Sir George the rebellion was almost over as the delay had given the Earl of Sussex time to muster his troops.

LATER HISTORY

After the siege of 1569, the castle and demesne lands continued to be leased by the Bowes family, with the rest of the estate being rented out by the Crown. Little or nothing was done to repair the castle. In 1574 the royal surveyors reported that many of the buildings were 'much decayed... in the floors, roofs, lead and in gutters.'

In 1603 James I gave the castle to his favourite Robert Carr, Earl of Somerset. In 1615, following Somerset's disgrace, the estate was transferred to the Prince of Wales who sold it to the City of London in 1626.

In 1630 it was resold to Sir Henry Vane. Sir Henry made Raby Castle his main residence and dismantled Barnard to use its materials in an extensive rebuilding programme there. An anonymous pamphleteer commented: 'O Misery! Can £100 worth of lead, iron, wood and stone be worth more than a castle which might have been a receptacle for a king and his whole train?'

By 1636 the land inside the castle walls was being used as a meadow for the growing of hay. Orders were made by the borough court that there was to be no building in the outer moat or the removal of stones from the walls, but these orders were soon ignored. By 1728, the time of the first engraving of the castle by the Buck brothers, it was already a gutted shell.

In 1952, Lord Barnard of Raby, the eventual owner of the estate, placed the Inner, Middle and Town wards in the guardianship of the Ministry of Works. From 1974 to 1982 a programme of excavation was carried out to reveal the foundations and something of the castle's development. The castle is now in the care of English Heritage.

EGGLESTONE ABBEY

INTRODUCTION

❖

EGGLESTONE ABBEY was founded in 1195 for a small group of Premonstratensian canons. Throughout the abbey's history the canons struggled against poverty and raids by the Scots. After the Dissolution, the abbey buildings were bought by Robert Strelly, who converted then into a home for himself and his family. A mere twenty years later, however, the buildings were in a poor state of repair. This gradual decline continued until, in the late nineteenth century, much of the abbey was pulled down and the stone used at nearby Rokeby Hall.

Egglestone Abbey, an engraving after a drawing by Thomas Hearne, 1782. Note the farmhouse in the east range still inhabited, and the north transept, not demolished until the end of the nineteenth century

TOUR AND
DESCRIPTION

❖

A fifteenth-century manuscript illustration of monks at their stalls in the 'choir'

Egglestone Abbey was built on land given to the canons by Ralph de Multon. The site was chosen for its seclusion, the local supply of stone and its proximity to water. Construction began in the twelfth century, with the church built first, as was the usual practice on monastic sites. The canons lived in temporary quarters until the domestic ranges were completed, sometime in the early thirteenth century. From the mid-thirteenth century the church was widened, the walls raised and the roofline altered, possibly because the size of the community had increased.

Monasteries were largely self-sufficient and Egglestone would originally have had an outer court, filled with agricultural and industrial buildings. The only survival is the Abbey Mill, now largely ruinous and best seen in early paintings of the abbey. The whole site was bounded by a precinct wall controlled by a gatehouse.

THE ABBEY CHURCH

You enter the site facing the side of the church.

The abbey church was used for worship by lay people as well as the canons. Because of this, the building was divided into separate areas by a series of screens to give the canons complete privacy.

At the west end is the nave, used by the lay congregation. The canons worshipped at the east end of the church, in the choir, usually sited underneath the crossing tower. There are a number of graves in this area, notably the 'table' tomb of Sir Rafe

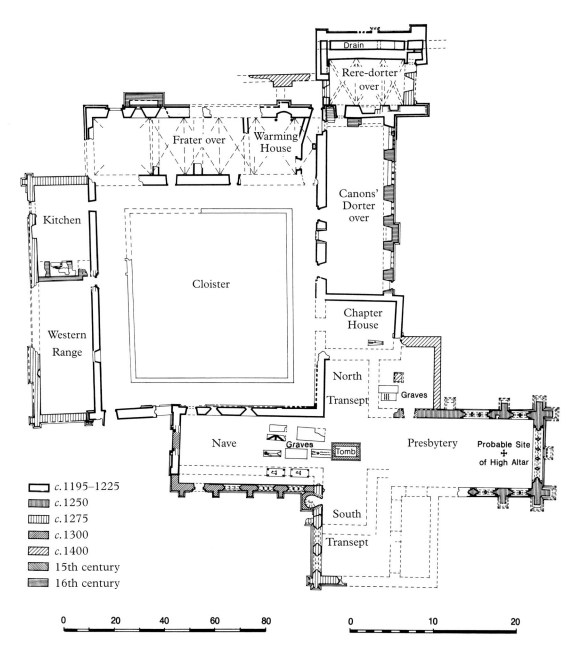

Drain

Rere-dorter over

Frater over

Warming House

Canons' Dorter over

Kitchen

Cloister

Chapter House

North Transept

Graves

Western Range

Nave

Graves

Tomb

Presbytery

Probable Site ✝ of High Altar

South Transept

☐	c.1195–1225
▥	c.1250
▦	c.1275
▨	c.1300
▧	c.1400
▥	15th century
▤	16th century

0   20   40   60   80

0   10   20

Bowes and that of Thomas Rokeby. Although generally reluctant to have laity buried in their churches, exceptions were made for founders and patrons. A descendant of the Rokebys commented that it was 'a great steppe towards heaven to have . . . burialls in those places and among those persons.'

At the east end is the presbytery, the site of the main, or high, altar. Here there are two sets of aumbries and piscinas, one in the east wall and one in the south wall. Aumbries are cupboards used to store the communion vessels, while piscinas were used to wash the vessels after a service.

Most of the north transept was still standing at the end of the nineteenth century. High up in the north wall was a round-headed doorway for the night-stairs. At midnight the canons would have been called to worship in a service called 'matins'; the night-stairs

❖ THE PREMONSTRATENSIANS ❖

❖ Canons are ordained priests who live a communal life, in contrast to monks who are not necessarily priests. The Premonstratensian Order was founded by St Norbert in 1120, at Prémontré in north-eastern France. They were known as 'white canons' because of the white habits they wore. Norbert wanted to create a stricter and more religious way of life for canons, and the lives of the canons were austere and frugal, based around a strict timetable of prayer, work and study. Long hours were spent in silence, with conversation only permitted at certain times and in certain places.

❖ The minimum number of canons needed to found a house was the apostolic number of twelve, plus the abbot, the head of the monastery. They were helped by lay brothers, who were not canons, but who shared the monastic life. There were also lay servants to help with manual work, and some novices, or trainees.

❖ Discipline was enforced by the rule of the order, but each monastery was also in an area known as a 'circary'. Each year, two abbots would visit the houses in their area and report back to the abbot of Prémontré. There would also be visits from the abbot of the 'mother house' where the canons originally came from. Punishments ranged from repeating one psalm and receiving one 'correction', given to those who were late for meals or forgot to change their clothes at the proper time, to expulsion for more serious offences.

allowed them to come straight from their beds to the church. A chapel was added to the transept in the fifteenth century. John Mitchell and his wife, probably benefactors of the abbey, are buried here.

The south transept had an eastern aisle containing two chapels. The stair turret was probably added in the fifteenth century. The doorway was put through an earlier archway. This may have been intended to lead to a wider nave, but this alteration never took place.

The church was probably only partly glazed and entirely unheated. Any decoration, such as wall-paintings and carving in wood and stone, would not have been elaborate as the order was very strict.

THE CLOISTER

The word 'cloister' comes from the Latin word '*claustrum*' meaning door-lock or bolt. This was the private area for the canons and was used for writing, study and meditation. The cloister consisted of four enclosed alleyways around a central garden or 'garth'. Most cloisters were originally open to the weather and must have been cold and cheerless in winter.

The alley against the church was traditionally used as the study area. The Premonstratensians were not a learned order, but the canons were expected to spend part of their time in study. There were probably desks

of wood or stone built into the walls, and a bench.

The east alley was usually used as a library. Small monastic houses had very few books; fifty would have been a large library, and many communities had fewer than a dozen. These were generally kept in cupboards or in the thickness of the cloister wall.

The alley opposite the church normally contained the 'laver' or washing place. This was a long rectangular wooden or stone trough

Looking toward the site of the high altar, with the tomb of Sir Rafe Bowes in the foreground

The remains of the abbey church, with the east range in the background

provided with piped water. The alley could also be used as a laundry, fitted up with wooden tubs and strung with washing lines.

Cloister gardens were often cultivated in some way, usually as formal gardens.

East Range

The chapter house was used for daily meetings. The name comes from the practice of starting the meetings with a reading of a chapter from the rules of the order. The canons sat on wall benches while the abbot had a seat against the east wall. There would be a lectern, or reading desk, in the centre. Meetings could be very lively, but sometimes very trying. The Premonstratensian abbot Adam of Dryburgh commented that 'there is too little love and tenderness in those sitting round, no pity or compassion whatever in the superior presiding,

but there is very great discomfort and unrest in my heart as I sit there'. In the corner there is a grave slab, probably that of an abbot, who were often buried in the chapter house.

Most of the monastic features of the dormitory block were swept away in the sixteenth-century conversion of the building, when the walls were raised and a third storey added. The ground floor was originally the parlour, where talking was permitted for limited periods. The day stairs, usually built against the chapter house, provided access to the dormitory on the first floor.

The canons slept in the dormitory. Early dormitories were a single open room, but later examples were often divided into cubicles using wooden screens. The canons slept on low beds with straw mattresses. St Benedict's Rule stated that 'for bedding, let this suffice: a mattress, a blanket, a coverlet and a pillow'.

At the end of the parlour is a small vaulted room. This may have been an early warming room, used before the north range was completed, or an infirmary. Infirmaries were used by old and sick members of the community and for periodical bleedings, thought to be good for the health.

At the back of the room is a single latrine, and a tall drain for the latrines of the floor above. There was another latrine opposite, but the doorway to this was blocked during the sixteenth century.

On the floor above are the main latrines. A number of wooden seats, possibly within individual cubicles, were positioned over the drain. The latrines were flushed by Thorsgill Beck which runs behind the building. Despite the use of running water, latrine drains would have to cleaned out by hand from time to time. Faeces were used as a fertilizer and it is possible that drains were allowed to build up deliberately for this purpose. Pottery urinals were also used to collect urine for use in tanning and the production of vellum, the material used in monastic books.

NORTH RANGE

The ground floor of this range was vaulted; corbels which supported the stone vault can be still be seen projecting from the walls.

The warming room would have been the only room in the monastery

❖ THE MONASTIC DIET ❖

The canons were strict vegetarians. Meals consisted of bread, cheese, vegetables, beans and cereals, with extra dishes, known as 'pittances', of fish and eggs on special occasions.

In winter it was usual to have one meal a day, usually around 2 p.m., but in summer there were two. 'Prandium', the main meal, was eaten around 12 p.m. and another meal, known as 'cena' would be taken at 5 or 5.30 p.m. It was felt that in the northern climate, this allowance was too frugal, and a drink was added, probably of beer, to be had in the evenings in winter and mid-afternoon in summer. In the thirteenth century there were attempts to allow two meals in winter.

BRITISH LIBRARY

The cellarer with his keys, sneakily having a secret cup of wine

Most food was produced by the canons on their own land. They grew vegetables and fruit, and herbs were grown in special gardens known as 'herbaria'. Most monastic sites had at least one fishpond, and the canons at Egglestone could also catch fish in the river, using weirs and fishtraps. Monasteries usually farmed sheep and cattle and sold the meat. Large monasteries had separate farms known as 'granges', but because Egglestone was so poor it probably only farmed the estate around the abbey, leasing out its more distant land. What could not be produced on the abbey's lands was bought at local fairs and markets and stored beneath the refectory by the cellarer, who was responsible for provisions.

with a fire, other than the infirmary and the kitchen. The fire was kept alight during the winter months, from November to Good Friday. The two narrow columns would have supported a hood over the fire.

The other rooms were used to store supplies. The chimney breast at the back of the building was added in the sixteenth century when the room was converted into a hall for the Strellys' house.

On the upper floor was the refectory, or dining room, reached by a set of stairs, somewhere near the west end. Refectories were usually on the ground floor, but canons often had their refectory at first-floor level, above a vaulted basement, to resemble the upper room in which Christ and his disciples celebrated the Last Supper. The refectory would have been simply furnished with trestle tables and benches.

At the furthest end from the doorway was a raised platform, or dais, where the abbot and senior officers sat. Set against the wall, near the upper end, was a pulpit from which a member of the abbey would read an appropriate passage from the Bible or other religious work during meals.

WEST RANGE

The west range, originally a two-storey building, contained the abbot's rooms at the south end and guest accommodation at the north end. As a small and remote house, it is unlikely that Egglestone had many visitors, but it was still expected to offer hospitality. The rules of the order stated that 'in every church of the order hospitality shall be observed and alms shall be distributed according to the resources of the place'.

Although there is a fireplace in the north of the building, it is unlikely that this was the original kitchen, but was converted into such during the sixteenth century. Monastic kitchens were normally built outside the cloister ranges because of the risk of fire, but would have been connected to the refectory by a short passage. The kitchen at Egglestone would probably been to the north, taking advantage of the running water supplied by the beck.

The abbey seen from the other bank of the River Tees

HISTORY

❖

The Abbey of St Mary and St John the Evangelist was founded between 1195 and 1198. None of the foundation charters survive, so it is difficult to know who the founder was. The most likely candidate is Ralph de Multon, who gave his lands at Egglestone to the canons. However, he only rented these lands from Ralph de Lenham, and a document shows he had to pay a fine of 15 marks. The date of this event is so close to the establishment of the abbey that it seems likely that they are connected.

The canons usually numbered fifteen, but several were the vicars of parish churches. A list of the brethren from 1491 shows that only the abbot and six canons were continually in residence, with eight others serving in churches. A number of canons also served as chantry priests. Chantries were personal chapels, usually founded by wealthy persons, where masses and prayers could be said for them. In 1275, John of Brittany, Earl of Richmond, gave his lands at Multon to the abbey on condition that the monastery gave him six canons to celebrate divine service in his castle for ever, except in time of war, when they were to perform the services in the abbey church.

In a charter of c.1205, Gilbert de Leya gave the manor of Kilvington to the community for the support of nine more canons. In 1248, Gilbert's son Philip brought an action in the king's court against the abbey, claiming that the abbot had refused to admit the new canons he had chosen to replace the original nine. The abbot produced Gilbert's charter which revealed no reference to the right to choose new canons. Philip argued that a charter drawn up by a former abbot, Nicholas, backed his claims. This charter was said to have no value as it had been made without the agreement of the chapter, and the jury ruled in favour of the abbot. Philip didn't give up, and in 1251 he forced the abbot to acknowledge that eight canons and a clerk should pray for the souls of Philip and his family in the abbey church forever. On the death of each canon he was allowed to nominate a replacement.

Poverty

Egglestone was very poor and struggled to maintain the minimum number of twelve canons. The abbey was so small that early in the thirteenth century the abbot of Prémontré held an enquiry to see if it should be reduced to the status of a priory. It retained its abbatial status, however.

Various archbishops of York tried to help the abbey by authorising the 'appropriation' of churches. If monasteries were given a parish church they received a pension from it, but if they appointed one of their own members to act as parish priest in that church, they would receive or 'appropriate' all its revenues. The abbey was allowed to appropriate a number of churches, including that of Great Ouseburn, given to the canons in 1348 by Sir Thomas Rokeby as compensation for damage done by the royal army before the battle of Neville's Cross.

Money was also donated by pilgrims. In 1398, as an incentive to visit the abbey, Pope Boniface VIII

Engraving of the abbey ruins in 1787

NORTH YORKSHIRE COUNTY RECORD OFFICE

offered an indulgence (absolution of sins) to anyone visiting on the principal religious feast days of the year. Money was also bequeathed to the canons. In 1421, Thomas Greenwood, a canon of York, left 26s 8d to the abbey to pray for his soul.

But the finances of the abbey were still so bad that it was often excused from paying taxes to the king. In 1496, they were noted as exempt 'on account of their notorious poverty'. Built close to the Scottish border, the abbey and its lands were vulnerable to attack. The Scots ravaged Yorkshire in 1315 and the canons' losses were so serious that their taxes were reduced from £63 to £30. In 1327 it was reported that their lands and goods had been so 'destroyed, burned and wasted by frequent invasions of the Scots' that 'nothing taxable is found in this place from which any tenth can be demanded or raised'.

LIFE IN THE ABBEY

There are few details of general life at Egglestone, but there are records of visitations from 1478 to 1502 by Bishop Redman. In 1478, he found little to complain of, except that some of the canons were lax in getting up for matins and that silence was not properly observed. In 1482, 1488 and 1494 the bishop only found fault with the canons for not keeping silence and for not wearing their cloaks at proper times. In 1497,

however, one of the canons had taken part in a quarrel which had led to a man's death. Although not directly responsible, he was banished to Halesowen Abbey for seven years, but seems to have returned by 1500. Another canon was also punished for involvement in the quarrel, although he had done his best to calm things down. The bishop forbad the canons to go out without permission, an order he repeated in 1500, adding that none were to carry long knives either inside or outside the abbey. The last recorded visitation, in 1502, revealed many serious defects and the canons were ordered to stop quarrelling and not to leave the abbey without permission.

A priest saying mass

There are two other interesting incidents we know about which reveal something of the tensions that could arise in self-contained communities such as monastic houses. Around 1285, a letter was sent to three English abbots claiming that the abbot of Egglestone was unfit to hold his position. Commissioners were immediately sent to investigate and found that the whole scandal had been made up by three canons. Of these, the chief offender was sentenced to be banished to 'some far distant church of the order'. The second was sent to Torre Abbey in Devon, while the third went to Prémontré to beg for pardon. The abbot considered that the latter had been let off lightly, with a penance

An early nineteenth-century engraving of the abbey church

which involved fasting on bread and water every sixth day for seven years and repeating one psalter and receiving one correction every week for that period.

In 1309 Abbot William resigned, possibly under pressure. He was treated very badly by his successor and the other canons, who eventually expelled him from the abbey. The abbots of Dale and Easby were sent to Egglestone to investigate. Despite finding some fault lay with the ex-abbot, they tried to persuade the canons to take him back or place him in Welbeck Abbey at their expense. The canons refused to do either. The abbot of Welbeck would not accept him without payment and two or three years passed before he found at home at Torre Abbey.

THE SUPPRESSION OF THE MONASTERY

After Henry VIII's break with the Pope, monasteries with an annual value of less than £200 were suppressed under the Act of 1536. In 1535, the king's commissioners had valued all monasteries, and recorded the net income of Egglestone at only £36 7s 2d, making it the poorest of the Premonstratensian houses in England. However, the Act also allowed the king to spare any houses he saw fit. Egglestone was exempted and refounded on 30 January 1537. Soon afterwards, however, larger abbeys began to be suppressed and on 5 January 1540 Egglestone surrendered to the king's commissioners. The last abbot, Thomas Shepherd, was given a pension of £13 6s 8d, his subprior, Robert Redshaw, £4, six priests £2 and the subdeacon £1 6s 8d.

LATER HISTORY

In 1548 the site was granted to Robert Strelly, who converted the buildings into a residence. The property remained in the family until the seventeenth century, but the building was neglected and seems to have been in a poor state as early as 1565 when Rafe Rokeby complained of its 'utter ruine and desolation' and that 'the ancestors of the howses of Bowes and Rokeby lye without the doores in the demesnes of Eggleston Abbey, where yett their gravestones appeare old and weatherbeaten'.

By 1770 Sir Thomas Robinson had sold it to John Morritt of Robeky, a noted traveller and classical scholar. Around this time the traveller and diarist John Byng, Viscount Torrington, visited the abbey and wrote that 'these ruins are entirely neglected, and choked up by weeds and nettles'. In 1905 the Rev. J. F. Hodgson recorded the destruction and removal of part of the cloister arcade and the north

transept in the late nineteenth century. The stones were used to pave the stable yard of Rokeby Hall. In 1925, Major Henry Edward Morritt placed the ruins in the guardianship of the state and Egglestone Abbey is now in the care of English Heritage.

The abbey ruins at sunset

BOWES CASTLE
TOUR AND DESCRIPTION

❖

B OWES CASTLE stands on the site of a Roman fort. First built in the twelfth century, it is a strong defensive tower, constructed to withstand the frequent Scottish raids which plagued the North. In 1171, the castle passed into the hands of the Crown, which strengthened its defences, but to little effect. By the early fourteenth century, the Scots had reduced the castle to ruins.

Bowes Castle lies in the north-west corner of the Roman fort of *Lavatrae*, built here to guard the road across the Pennines. The strategic importance of the site was recognised by the Normans, who built the castle here around 1136. Only the tower remains, but there were probably and inner and outer courtyards as well, with buildings built of wood. The moat may have marked the edge of the inner courtyard, but at present it is impossible to give a precise function, date or extent to the moat.

Bowes is a type of castle known as a 'keep', designed to hold all the accommodation necessary for a lord and his household within a single defensive tower. Protection was given by the extremely thick walls, and by archers stationed on the battlements on the roof and through the arrow slits in the walls. There were probably square turrets at each corner.

The keep of Bowes Castle

Across the east face of the tower are the remains of the forebuilding. It was usual for a keep to have only one entrance, at first or second floor level, reached by a flight of stairs within a defensive forebuilding. At the head of the stairs was a small hallway, which could be protected by a portcullis. There were two rooms beneath the hallway, probably used for storage, and possibly another room overhead. In many keeps this room was used as a chapel. Opposite the hallway there was usually a porter's lodge. The entrance could be further protected by a drawbridge with a pit beneath it. The door was secured by wooden bars, held in long slots in the thickness of the wall.

There is a well at the north corner of the forebuilding. The well was usually in the basement, so that if the castle came under attack, the occupants still had access to water. The well may have been dug at a later date, or is further evidence of an inner court surrounding the keep.

INTERIOR

The entrance to the keep is now in the south wall, through what was originally an arrow slit. Inside are two residential floors and a basement joined by a spiral staircase. There are also a number of small rooms in the thickness of the walls. The whole building was divided into two unequal parts by a thick crosswall, which supported a double-pitch roof, forming an 'M' shape.

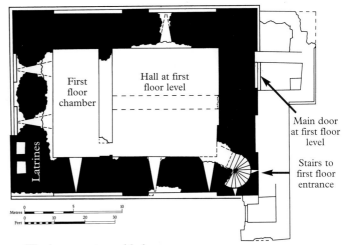

The basement provided a secure storage space for valuable foodstuffs and weapons. Projecting for the walls are the supports for a vaulted ceiling, added in the thirteenth or fourteenth century.

On the first floor was the hall – the main living and eating room – and a smaller private bedchamber for the lord. To the left of the main entrance was a kitchen with a round-backed fireplace. To the right is a small chamber, possibly used to store food and drink. A third door off the hall leads to a 'garderobe', or latrine. There is a second garderobe next to it, with private access from the lord's chamber. All the garderobes emptied into a pit at the base of the wall, visible from the outside.

The second floor would have probably held further accommodation, but we cannot be sure of its exact function from what remains.

HISTORY

❖

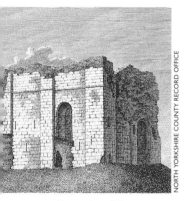

Engraving of Bowes Castle, 1775

THE ROMAN FORT was first built during Agricola's campaigns in northern Britain in the late first century AD. The earthen and timber ramparts were replaced by stone in the early second century and the fort occupied until the fourth century.

The Norman castle was started in about 1136 by Alan, Count of Brittany, who held the nearby castle and earldom of Richmond. After the death of Alan's son, Earl Conan the Little, ownership passed to the Crown.

The king, Henry II, immediately set about strengthening the castle. In 1173, the Scots attacked the castle and in 1174 money was spent on repairs. At the same time 'bulwarks', an earthen rampart, was built around the tower, in preparation for an invasion by King William the Lion of Scotland.

Under King John, custody of the castle was given to Robert de Vipont in 1203–4. John stayed here on his way to Carlisle in 1206–7 and again in 1212. He is also known to have imprisoned his niece Eleanor here.

In 1232, the castle and estates were granted to the Duke of Brittany, but a few years later were transfered to Henry III's half-brother, William de Valence. After his death in 1241 the castle and manor were granted for life to Peter of Savoy, the king's uncle and Earl of Richmond. When Edward II granted ownership to John de Scargill in 1322 there was much local resentment, and the castle was besieged and captured by tenants of the Earl of Richmond.

In the years 1314 to 1322 the North was devastated by the Scots, and by 1325 the castle was reported to be in ruins. In 1340–41 it was reported to be 'weak and worth nothing' and 'ruins, untenable and of no value'. After John de Scargill's death in 1361, the castle reverted to the Crown. In 1444, the property was granted to the powerful Nevill family, who held it until 1471 when it once again reverted to the Crown. James I sold it in the early seventeenth century, and any military worth that remained was destroyed during the Civil War. The castle is now in the care of English Heritage.